The REALLY WICKED KIDS' JOKE BOOK

The REALLY WICKED KIDS' JOKE BOOK

A fantastic collection of utterly stupid, corny and altogether pointless jokes that you will love inflicting on everyone you meet !

Collected and Illustrated by

Peter Coupe

ARCTURUS

Published by Arcturus Publishing Limited
For Bookmart Limited

Registered Number 2372865
Trading as Bookmart Limited
Desford Road
Enderby
Leicester
LE9 5AD

This edition published 2000

Printed and bound in Finland
© Peter Coupe / Arcturus Publishing Limited

ISBN 1 84193 017 2

Contents...

ALIEN ATTACK

What should you do with a green alien?

Wait until it's ripe!

What do you call an alien with two heads ?

A two-headed alien !

What do aliens do with humans they find in space ships ?

Put them in the larder - they keep tinned food for emergencies !

What should you do if you find a green alien ?

Wait until it's ripe !

Why do aliens have seven
fingers on each hand ?

**Because otherwise they
would have two empty
fingers in each glove !**

Where do aliens live ?

In green houses !

What lights do aliens switch on every Saturday ?

Satellites !

What game do aliens play to while away
the hours in deep space ?

Moonopoly !

Where do alien children
go in the evenings ?

Rocket and Roll concerts !

What are wealthy aliens members of ?

The Jet Set !

Where do aliens go to study their GCSEs ?

High School (Very High School) !

Why do aliens never starve in space ?

**Because they always know where to find a Mars, a
Galaxy and a Milky Way !**

What do evil aliens eat for lunch ?

Beans on toast - (Human Beans on toast) !

Why are aliens good for the environment ?

Because they are green !

What do aliens have to do before they can drive a rocket
at twice the speed of light in deep space ?

Reverse it out of the garage !

What do aliens call junk food ?

Unidentified Frying Objects !

How do you know when
aliens are envious ?

Easy - they turn green !

What sort of sweets to Martians eat ?

Martian mallows !

Where do aliens go to study rocket science ?

Mooniversity !

How do you know when an alien is homesick ?

He just moons about all over the place !

What do you give a sick alien ?

Planetcetamol !

What do giant space monsters play to relax ?

Squash !

How do you contact someone who lives on Saturn ?

Give them a ring !

What is the quickest way to get an alien baby to sleep ?

Rocket !

Alien School Report

Music   He loves the Planet Suite by Holst !

Chemistry   Blew off one of his heads making
                 rocket fuel !

Martian   KLargin SCRungjlkfr TTTTugt KLMgg
                 FRelOOmmMw~We TTrRaaakk !

Maths   Can count up to seventeen using the
                 fingers on his left hand !

Space   Takes a bite out of the Milky Way
                 every time he goes there on a school trip !

What do you call an alien girl band ?

The Space Girls !

What do you call a mad alien ?

A Lunar-tic !

What game do nasty
aliens play with Earth
space ships ?

Shuttlecocks !

What is the name of
the planet inhabited by
video recorders ?

Planet of the Tapes !

What ticket do you ask for to go there for a holiday?

Return to the Planet of the Tapes!

Which side of a spaceship passes
closest to the planets?

The Outside!

Why did the impressionist crash through the ceiling?

He was taking off a rocket taking off!

What does an alien gardener do with his hedges?

Eclipse them every Spring!

Why did the alien buy a pocket computer ?

So he could work out how many pockets he has !

How can you tell if a computer is disgruntled ?

It will have a chip on its shoulder !

How do you get directions in deep space ?

Askeroid !

Where do aliens keep fish they capture
from other planets ?

In a planetarium !

Why did the alien school have no computers ?

Because someone ate all the apples !

What do evil aliens grind up to make a hot drink ?

Coffee beings !

What do you call an alien who travels
through space on a ketchup bottle ?

A flying saucer !

Why did the attendant turn space ships
away from the lunar car park ?

It was a full moon !

How does a Martian know he's attractive ?

When bits of metal stick to him !

What do you call a space ship made from cow pats ?

A Pooh F O !

Where do alien space ship pilots go to learn how to fly in
the darkness of outer space ?

Night school !

What do you call a sad space ship ?

An unidentified crying object !

What does the alien from planet X
use to smooth her nails ?

The X Files, of course !

Do space ships like this crash very often?

Only the once!

Why are alien gardeners so good?

Because they have green fingers!

What do alien children do on Halloween?

They go from door to door dressed as humans!

How do you know if there is an alien in your house ?

There will be a spaceship parked in the garden !

How do you communicate with aliens out in deep space ?

You have to shout really loudly !

How do you tell if an alien is embarrassed ?

They blush - and their cheeks go purple !

How do you catch a Venusian mega mouse ?

In a Venusian mega mouse-trap !

✎

What do you give a sick alien ?

Paracetamoons !

✎

Where do aliens do their shopping ?

In a greengrocers !

✎

Why do some aliens make their space ships out of twisted planks of wood ?

So they can travel at warp speed !

✎

Who is in love with the alien james Bond ?

Miss Mooneypenny !

Where do aliens go for holidays ?

Lanzarocket !

Where do aliens put on their cakes ?

Mars - ipan !

Who is the aliens' favourite robot
cartoon character ?

Tin - Tin !

Why was the robot rubbing its joints with a video ?

Because it was a video of Grease !

What is a robot's favourite chocolate ?

Whole Nut !

Where are parts for robots made ?

In Bolton, Knutsford and Leeds !

What do you give a robot who fancies a light snack ?

Some 60 watt bulbs !

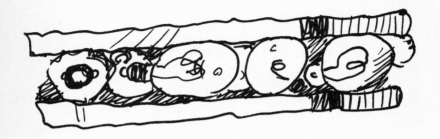

What did the teacher give the alien monster for lunch ?

Class 4B !

What sort of music do robots like best ?

Steel band music !

Who do robots vote for in a General Election ?

Tinny Blair !

How do you know when a robot
has been in your fridge ?

There are footprints in the butter !

How do you invite a robot to a party ?

Send round a tinvitation !

What firework do aliens like best ?

Rockets !

What did the robot say to the petrol pump ?

Take your finger out of your ear when I'm talking to you !

What is an alien's favourite TV programme ?

Blind date - it's the only way they can get a human girlfriend !

What do you call computer controlled sandpaper ?

Science Friction !

If you get lost in space - who should
you ask for directions ?

**An alien hairdresser -
they know all the short cuts !**

✐

If an alien leaves his chewing gum orbiting
the Earth - what
do you call it ?

A Chew - F - O !

✐

Your son will make an
excellent rocket pilot !

Why do you say that ?

He has nothing but
space between his ears !

✐

Why do steel robots have so many friends ?

I suppose they must have magnetic personalities !

What do daleks drink ?

Exterminade !

What do aliens put on their toast ?

Mars - malade !

Where is the smelliest part of an alien spaceship ?

The Com - poooh - ter !

Why did the alien paint his spaceship
with sugar and vinegar ?

He wanted a sweet and sour saucer !

How do you tip an alien spaceship over ?

Rocket !

What did the greedy alien say when he
landed on a new planet ?

Take me to your larder !

What dance can you see in the night sky ?

The Moon Walk !

Why did the football manager want to get
in touch with the alien ?

Because he knew where all the shooting stars were !

What did the mummy robot say to her children ?

Look before you bleep !

Why was the young robot so happy ?

Because he didn't have a chip on his shoulder !

Where does the alien gardener keep his tools ?

In an astro - hut !

Where do Martians go to see a movie?

Cine - mars !

Knock, knock,
Who's there ?
Jupiter
Jupiter Who ?
Jupiter spaceship on my lawn ?

What is worse than finding a 12 legged Venusian
mega - maggot in your apple ?

**Finding half a 12 legged Venusian
mega - maggot in your apple !**

What did the referee book the alien for ?

Hand ball, Hand ball, Hand ball, Hand ball....

What do aliens use to go up and down ?

Stairs !

Where did they put the alien who stole a field
full of rhubarb ?

In Custardy !

What is green and very noisy ?

An alien with a drum kit !

Who was the first man on the moon ?

A Spaceman !

What did one rocket say to the other ?

I wish I could stop smoking !

I don't know what to buy my pal, the
space alien, for his birthday ?!

How about 5 pairs of slippers !

Why do astronauts never eat after take off ?

Because they have just had a big launch !

SCHOOL SCREAMS

When are skipping ropes like schoolchildren?

When they are taught!

Why did the teacher leave his job ?

He was head hunted !

Blenkinsop, why are you looking in lost property ?

*My granny moved house last week and I can't
remember where she lives now !*

Surely you can remember what happened in 1066 ?

It's alright for you, sir, you were there !

Sarah. I think your father has been helping you with your homework !

No, Miss, he did it all by himself !

Today we are going to look for the lowest common denominator...

Haven't they found that yet, my dad says they were looking for that when he was at school !

Blenkinsop - you deserve a hundred lines for this homework !

Ah, but it wouldn't be fair on the rest of the class if I always got what I deserved would it, sir !

Parent - Do you think my son will make a good Arctic explorer ?

Teacher - I would think so, most of his marks are below zero !

✎

Teacher - You should have been here at 9 o'clock this morning !

Parent - Why, did something happen ?

✎

Please don't talk while you are doing your exam !

It's alright, miss, we're not doing the exam - just talking !

Science teacher - Name two liquids that don't freeze...

Mary - Coffee and tea !

History teacher - Who shot King Harold ?

Blenkinsop - My mum told me never to tell tales !

Geography teacher - Where is Hadrian's wall ?

Blenkinsop - Where he left it !

Why are maths teachers no good at gardening ?

Because everything they plant grows square roots !

Did you hear about the maths teacher whose mistakes started to multiply ?

They took him away in the end !

Did you hear about
the two history
teachers who met
on television ?

**They were on
Blind Date !**

Did you hear about
the stupid P.E. teacher ?

**He was a
physical jerk !**

Susie, How do you make a milk shake ?

Take it to a scary film, Miss !

Blenkinsop, do you understand how important punctuation is ?

Yes, Miss, I always make sure I get to school on time !

Mark, how did Moses cut the sea in half ?

With a sea-saw ?

Wendy, when do you like school the best ?

During the school holidays, Sir !

What do skeleton teachers say at the start of the lesson ?

As there is nobody here we can start !

Brian, what is water ?

**A colourless liquid which turns black when
I put my hands in it !**

You, boy, which part of a fish weighs the most ?

The scales, sir ?

What do Atilla the Hun and Winnie the
Pooh have in common ?

The !

Smith, name me someone who has been round the globe ?

Terminator, Miss !

Who on earth is Terminator ?

My goldfish !!

Watson, shouldn't you wash your hands before you start your piano lesson ?

No, Miss, I only play on the black notes !

Carol, what is the difference between a policeman and a soldier ?

You can't dip a policeman into your boiled egg, Sir !

Now, Roger, if a half filled barrel of beer fell on someone, how badly hurt would they be?

Not at all if it was light ale, Miss !?

✎

Why are you putting in those ear plugs?

I've got to teach form 4B tennis, and they always make such a racket !

Now, can anyone tell me what Egyptian Kings
were buried with ?

Yes, Miss, they were buried with their Nammaforrs !

What is a Nammaforr ?

Knocking nails in !

Blenkinsop, how can
you prove that the
Earth is round ?

I didn't say it was, Sir !

What do you call a
teacher swearing ?

A Sir - Cuss !

What did you think
of your first day at
school Joe ?

**First ?! You mean I
have to go back again !**

What is the difference between frogspawn and school pudding ?

Frogspawn was once warm !

How can you tell if a teacher is in a good mood ?

Let me know if you ever find out !

Why are you always late for school ?

It's not my fault, you always ring the bell before I get here !

Why did the teacher make you take the chicken out of the classroom ?

He said he didn't want anyone to hear fowl language in his lesson !

Howard, which is the largest sea?

The Galax-sea!

What is a bunsen burner used for?

Setting fire to bunsens, Miss?

Sir, can we do some work on the Iron Age today?

**Well, I'm not certain, I'm a bit rusty on
that period of history!**

Smith, How would you hire a horse ?

Put a brick under each leg ?

Why did Cyclops
have to retire
from teaching ?

**He only had
one pupil !**

Why is your
homework late,
Bloggs ?

**Sorry, Miss,
my Dad is a
slow writer !**

Did you hear about the teacher who went
to a mind reader ?

She gave him his money back !

Blenkinsop, how do you get rid of varnish?

Just take out the 'R', Miss!

Smith, where do fish sleep?

On a waterbed?

Harry, what does it mean if I say
'Guten Morgen Herr Dresser'?

It means you've gone for a haircut!

Sally, what musical instrument do Spanish
fishermen play?

Cast - a - nets?

✎

Bill, which is heavier, a full moon or a half moon?

A half moon, because a full moon is lighter!

✎

Mary, how did you find the questions
in your English exam?

**Oh, I found the questions easily enough, it's the
answers I couldn't find!**

✎

Geoff, why are you eating with a knife?

Because my fork leaks!

Who invented fractions ?

Henry the eighth !

Ten cats were at the cinema; one walked out,
how many were left ?

None - they were all copycats !

Wally, what is a dumb waiter ?

Someone who gets all the orders mixed up, Sir ??

Sue, describe crude oil for me !

**Well, Sir, it is black and sticky and it floats on the sur-
face of water shouting 'knickers' !**

Joe, how many seconds are there in a year?

Twelve, Miss, January 2nd, February 2nd, March 2nd, April 2nd....

Flora, what is the most important tool we use in mathematics?

Multi - pliers!

Fred, where do most spiders live?

Crawley!

Did you hear about the two history teachers
who got married ?

They liked to sit at home talking about old times !

Where did the metalwork teacher meet his wife ?

In a bar !

What happened after the wheel was first invented ?

It caused a revolution !

Robert, why do doctors and nurses wear
masks in the operating theatre ?

So no-one will know who did it if they make a mistake !

How do archaeologists get into locked tombs ?

Do they use a skeleton key, Miss ?

I've just got a place in the school football team - the games teacher says I'm the main drawback !

Steven, why did Henry the eighth have so many wives ?

He liked to chop and change, Miss ?

Why did the very first chips not taste very nice ?

Because they were fried in ancient Greece !

Sarah, where would you find a gorilla ?

In a kitchen ?

Jane, what do you know about the Dead Sea ?

I didn't even know it had been poorly, Sir !

William, what is a fungi ?

A mushroom that likes having a good time ?

'John can't come to school today, because he has a cold.'

'Who am I speaking to ?'

'My father.'

Harry, spell mouse trap...

C. A. T. !

Where do vampire teachers train ?

Teacher Draining College !

Billy, what is a wombat ?

It's what you use to play Wom, Miss !

Carol, can you give me a sentence with deliberate in it ?

'My dad bought a new settee and tomorrow they are going to deliberate to our house !'

What do you call the teacher who
organises all the exams?

Mark!

Blenkinsop, I do wish you would pay a little attention!

I'm paying as little as I can, Sir!

Fred, how do fleas get from one animal to another ?

They itch hike !

Gloria, did you write this poem all by yourself ?

Yes, Miss !

Well, well, and I thought Shakespeare was a man !

John, what is the longest word in the
English dictionary ?

Elastic !

How do you work that out ?

It stretches !

James, give me a sentence with the word fascinate
in it !

**Fatty Perkins' coat has ten buttons, but he can
only fascinate of them !**

Howard, If I had 12 sausages in one hand, and 15 sausages in the other, how many sausages would I have altogether?

No idea, Miss, I'm a vegetarian!

Freda will make a good astronomer when she leaves school, as she is very good at staring into space for hours on end!

What makes you think that my son, Martin, is always playing truant?

Martin? There's no Martin in this school!

What do you call a man who keeps on talking when no-one is listening ?

Sir !

I hope I don't catch you cheating in the maths exam !

So do I, Miss !

Fred, what food do giraffe's eat ?

Neck - tarines !

Mary, why have you brought that fish into school ?

Because we will be practising scales in the music lesson !

Jim, why did Robin Hood steal from the rich ?

Because the poor didn't have anything worth stealing !

Florence, where were most English Kings
and Queens crowned ?

On the head ?!

✏

Robert, why have you been suspended from school ?

Because the boy next to me was smoking !

But if he was smoking, why were you suspended ??

Because I was the one who set fire to him !

✏

Ian, when was the Forth bridge constructed ?

After the first three had all fallen down ?

✏

Graham, what is a crane ?

A bird that can lift really heavy weights ?!

Philip, why do you always have two plates
of food for school dinner ?

It's important to have a balanced diet, Miss !

Mandy, do you have to come to school chewing gum ?

No, Sir, I can stay at home and chew it if your prefer !

Did you hear about the maths teacher
who was taken away ?

✎

Where were traitors beheaded ?

Just above the shoulders !

✎

Graham, what are net profits ?

What fishermen have left after paying the crew ?

✎

William, how do you make a Mexican chilli ?

Take him to the South Pole, Miss !

Mum: Do you say a little prayer before you
eat your school dinner ?

Son: Good heavens no - the food isn't that bad !

✎

George, you have had a very undistinguished career at
this school - have you ever been first in anything ?

Only the lunch queue, Miss !

✎

Why is the school cheese on toast hairy ?

**Because the cook dropped it on the floor
then wiped it on her jumper !**

How can bats fly without bumping into anything ?

They use their wing mirrors !

Sarah, give me a sentence with the word illegal in it !

My dad took me to the bird hospital the other day and we saw a sick sparrow and an illegal !

William, how fast does light travel ?

I don't know, Sir, it's already arrived by the time I wake up !

What do you give a sick bird ?

Tweetment !

How many maths teachers can you get in an empty Mini ?

Just one - after that it isn't empty any more !

Miriam, what is the hottest planet in our solar system ?

Mer - Curry !

Time to get up and go to school !

I don't want to go! Everyone hates me and I get bullied !

But you have to go - you're the headteacher !

Fred: Our teacher left last week and we all chipped in
to buy her a bottle of toilet water. It cost £15 !

**Jane: Wow, I would have given you a whole bucket
of water from my toilet for 50 pence !**

Your teacher says you're disgusting and
not fit to live with pigs !

What did you say ?

I stuck up for you, I said yes you are !

Teacher: Millie, why do you say that Moses wore a wig ?

Millie: Because sometimes he was seen with Aaron, and
sometimes without !

Pupil - Those eggs look a bit past their best !

School Cook - Don't blame me, I only laid the tables !

What do you call an American cartoonist ?

Yankee Doodle !

Blenkinsop, you could be in the school football team, if it weren't for two things !

What are they, Sir ?

Your feet !

BLENKINSOP'S FEET !

In South America, cowboys chase cattle
on horseback !

WOW ! I didn't know cows could ride at all !

Who was the fastest runner of all time ?

Adam, because he was first in the human race !

My dad baked some cakes, and said I have to
give one to my teacher !

**Gee ! I never realised just how much he
must hate your teacher !**

Blenkinsop - Why do birds fly South in the Winter ?

Because it is too far to walk !

What is a snake's favourite subject ?

Hissss-tory !

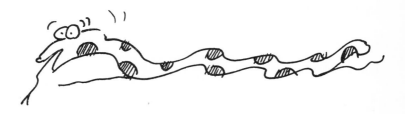

I told my dad I needed an encyclopedia for school !

What did he say ?

He said I could go on the bus like everyone else !

Head - You start on £20,000 a year, but go on to £24,000 after the first year.

Teacher - Oh ! Well, I'll come back in a year and start work then !

What does an elf do after school ?

Gnome work !

✎

**You have to be a really good whistler to
use the school toilets here !**

Why is that ?

The locks are all broken !

✎

If I cut a potato in two, I have two halves.
If I cut a potato in four, I have four quarters.
What do I have if I cut a potato in sixteen ?

Chips !

How did knights make chain mail?

From steel wool?

Why did the flea get thrown out of school?

He just wasn't up to scratch!

Why was the glow worm sad?

Because her children weren't very bright!

In this examination you will be allowed
15 minutes for each question !

Crikey, they sound like long questions !

What did the music teacher need a ladder for ?

Reaching the top notes !

Your son will be a good printer's assistant !

What makes you say that ?

He's exactly the right type !

Did you have any problems with your
French on your school trip to Paris ?

No, but the French certainly did !

Terry - how do you join the Police Force ?

Handcuff them together ?

John, name one use of Beech wood !

Making deck chairs ?

What is easy to get into, but
difficult to get out of ?

Trouble !

✎

My mum says the school beef pie is good for you
because it is full of iron !

That explains why it's so tough then !

✎

What was the blackbird doing in the school library ?

Looking for bookworms !

Mary, What do you think a pair of
crocodile shoes would cost ?

**That would depend on the size of your
crocodile's feet Miss !**

Fred, I told you to write 100 lines because your handwriting is so bad, but you have only done 75 !

**Sorry Miss, but my maths is just as
bad as my handwriting !**

Jim, what is 'won't' short for ?

Will not, Miss !

Very good. What is 'don't' short for ?

Er...Donut Miss ?

Harry, how would you fix a short circuit ?

Add some more wire to make it longer, Sir ?

Where do dim witches go ?

Spelling classes !

Well, Geoff, did you get a good position in the maths test yesterday ?

Yes, Sir, I was in front of a radiator, and next to the smartest person in the class !

What is the most important letter to a stick insect ?

The letter 'T' - without it he would be a sick insect !

Do you know a boy called Jim Wibley?

Yes, he sleeps next to me in Geography!

Michael can you name two inventions that have helped mankind to get up in the world?

... Yes, Miss, the stepladder and the alarm clock!

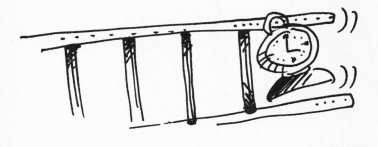

What do you call it when the Headteacher dosen't tell the truth about nits in his hair?

Head Lice!

How many teachers work at your new school Samantha?

About half of them!

Why was the teacher's head eleven inches long ?

Because if it was twelve inches it would be a foot !

What was Richard the Third's middle name ?

The !

You shouldn't play those notes on the piano !

Why not ?

You'll get into treble if you do !

Caroline, how many days of the week start
with the letter 'T' ?

Four; Tuesday,
Thursday,
Today and
Tomorrow !

The School Notice Board

Violin for sale - really cheap - no strings attached !

Dog free to good home - eats anything,
Loves children !

Why did the school orchestra have such
awful manners ?

Because it didn't know how to conduct itself !

What comes out of a teacher's wallet
at 100 miles an hour ?

Stirling Moth !

Table for sale, by Mr Wibley
with wooden legs !

On the school field trip a crab bit my toe !

Which one ?

I don't know, all crabs look the same to me !

CRAZY CROSSES

What do you get if you cross a
jogger with an apple pie?

Puff Pastry!

What do you get if you cross a sheep and a space ship ?

Apollo neck woolly jumpers !

What do you get if you cross a pig
with a naked person ?

Streaky bacon !

What do you get if you cross a box of
matches and a giant ?

The big match !

What do you get if you cross a kangaroo with
a skyscraper ?

A high jumper !

What do you get if you cross a road with a
safari park ?

Double yellow lions !

What do you get if
you cross an artist
with a policeman ?

A brush with the law !

What do you get if
you cross an overweight
golfer and a pair of very
tight trousers ?

A hole in one !

What do you get if you cross a plumber with
a field of cow pats?

The poohed piper!

What do you get if you cross an elephant
and a bottle of whisky?

Trunk and disorderly!

What do you get if you cross a flock
of sheep and a radiator?

Central bleating!

What do you get if you cross a skunk
and a pair of tennis rackets ?

Ping pong !

What do you get if you cross a pudding
and a cow pat ?

A Smelly Jelly !

What do you get if you cross a pig and
a box of itching powder ?

Pork scratching !

What do you get if you cross a bear with a freezer ?

A teddy brrrrr !

What do you get if
you cross a computer
with a vampire ?

**Something new
fangled !**

What do you get if
you cross a tin
opener, a vampire
and a cricket team ?

An opening bat !

What do you get if you cross a
cow with a grass cutter ?

A lawn mooer !

What do you get if you cross an
ice cream with a dog ?

Frost-bite !

What do you get if you cross a helicopter
with a cornish pasty ?

Something pie in the sky !

What do you get if you cross a pair of dogs with a
hairdresser ?

A shampoodle and setter !

What do you get if you cross a shoulder
bag with a Mallard ?

A ducksack !

What do you get if you cross a dinosaur with a dog ?

Tyrannosaurus Rex !

What do you get if you cross a football team with a
bunch of crazy jokers ?

Mad jester United !

What do you get if you cross a Viking
and a detective ?

Inspector Norse!

What do you get if you cross a large computer and a
beefburger ?

A Big Mac !

What do you get if
you cross an overheating
large computer with a
beefburger ?

A Big Mac and fries !

What do you get if
you cross a hat factory
and a field of cows ?

A pat on the head !

What do you get if you cross a mouse
and a bottle of olive oil ?

A squeak that oils itself !

What do you get if you cross a jogger
with an apple pie ?

Puff pastry !

What do you get if you cross a detective with a cat ?

A peeping Tom !

What do you get if you cross a TV programme
and a load of sheep ?

A flock-U-mentary !

What do you get if you cross a footballer
and a mythical creature ?

A centaur forward !

What do you get if you cross an actress and a glove
puppet ?

Sooty and Streep !

What do you get if you cross a pasty
and a scary film ?

A Cornish nasty !

What do you get if you cross a pig
and a part in a film ?

A ham roll !

What do you get if you cross a sports
reporter with a vegetable ?

A common tater !

What do you get if you cross a wireless with a hairdresser ?

Radio waves !

What do you get if you cross a hairdresser and a bucket of cement ?

Permanent waves !

What do you get if you cross a toadstool and a full suitcase ?

Not mushroom for your holiday clothes !

What do you get if you cross a dog with a vampire ?

A were - woof !

What do you get if you cross a bike and a rose ?

Bicycle petals !

What do you get if you cross an alligator
and King Midas ?

A croc of gold !

What do you get if you cross a tortoise and a storm ?

An 'I'm not in a hurry cane !'

What do you get if you cross a chicken with a pod ?

Chick peas !

What do you get if you cross a computer
with a potato ?

Micro chips !

What do you get if you cross a dog with a maze ?

A labyrinth !

What do you get if you cross a cow with a crystal ball ?

A message from the udder side !

What do you get if you cross a
crocodile with a camera ?

A snapshot !

What do you get if you cross a chicken
and an electricity socket ?

A battery hen !

What do you get if you cross a plank of wood
and a pencil ?

A drawing board !

What do you get if
you cross a dog
with a football game ?

Spot-The-Ball !

What do you get if
you cross a spider
with a computer ?

A web page !

What do you get if you cross a toilet with a
pop singer ?

Loo - Loo !

What do you get if you cross a frog
with a traffic warden ?

Toad away !

What do you get if you cross a flea
with some moon rock ?

A lunar - tick !

What do you get if you cross a vampire
and a circus entertainer ?

Something that goes straight for the juggler !

What do you get if you cross a snake
with a building site ?

A boa-constructor !

What do you get if you cross a parrot
with an alarm clock ?

Politics !

What do you get if you cross a bottle of
washing up liquid and a mouse ?

Bubble and squeak !

What do you get if you cross a mountain
and a baby ?

A cry for Alp !

What do you get if you cross a bunch
of flowers with some insects ?

Ants in your plants !

What do you get if you cross a bunch of flowers with a burglar ?

Robbery with violets !

What do you get if you cross a cow and a goat ?

Butter from a butter !

What do you get if you cross a pair of hiking boots and a parrot ?

A walkie-talkie !

What do you get if
you cross a
pen with
Napoleon's feet ?

**A footnote
in history !**

What do you get if
you cross a skunk
and a pair of
rubber boots ?

Smelly wellies !

What do you get if you cross a ghost
and an Italian restaurant ?

Spookhetti !

What do you get if you cross a cow
with an out of date map ?

Udderly lost !

What do you get if you cross a TV soap
and a rabbit colony ?

Burrow Nation Street !

What do you get if you cross a pelican and a zebra ?

Across the road safely !

What do you get if
you cross a bee
and a coach ?

A Buzzzz !

What do you get if
you cross a
monster and a
chicken ?

Free strange eggs !

What do you get if you cross a fish
and bad breath ?

Halibut - osis !

What do you get if you cross a
compass and a shellfish ?

A guided mussel !

What do you get if you cross a school
with a computer supplier ?

Floppy Desks !

What do you get if you cross a baby with soldiers ?

Infantry !

What do you get if you cross a very bent piece
of wood with a spaceship ?

Warp factor 7 !

What do you get if you cross a hairdresser,
a storyteller and a young horse ?

A pony tail !

What do you get if
you cross a
motorcycle and
a funny story ?

A Yamaha ha ha ha !

What do you get if you cross a leopard
and a bunch of flowers ?

A beauty spot !

What do you get if you cross a biscuit with a car tyre ?

Crumbs !

What do you get if you cross a rabbit
and an aeroplane ?

The hare force !

What do you get if you cross a
Welshman with a problem ?

A Dai - lemma !

What do you get if you cross a pub and a steelworks?

An iron bar!

What do you get if you cross a cow
and a jogging machine?

A milk shake!

What do you get if you cross a book
and a pound of fat?

Lard of the Rings!

What do you get if you cross a
newsreader and a toad ?

A croaksman !

What do you get if you cross a
ghost and a newsreader ?

A Spooksman !

What do you get if you cross a
suitcase with a filbert ?

A nut case !

What do you get if you cross a donkey
and Christmas ?

Muletide greetings !

What do you get if you cross the devil
and an anagram ?

Santa !

What do you get if you cross a Shakespeare
play and 3 eggs ?

Omelette !

What do you get if you cross a Shakespeare play
and a pig ?

A Ham omelette !

What do you get if you cross a Shakespeare
play and a vampire ?

Bat breath !

What do you get if you cross an
Eskimo and an ex-boyfriend ?

The cold shoulder !

What do you get if you cross a penguin and an elk ?

Chocolate moose !

What do you get if you cross a chemical and a bicycle ?

Bike carbonate of soda !

What do you get if you cross a skeleton,
a feather and a joke book ?

Rib ticklers !

What do you get if you cross a
skeleton and a garden spade ?

Skullduggery !

What do you get if you cross a skeleton and a dog ?

An animal that buries itself !

What do you get if you cross a
skeleton and a tumble drier ?

Bone dry clothes !

What do you get if you cross
a fish and a Yamaha ?

A motor pike !

What do you get if you cross a radio music presenter with Match of the Day ?

D D D D D D D D D D D D D D J !

What do you get if you cross teeth with candy ?

Dental floss !

What do you get if you cross
a Spice Girl with a pudding ?

A Jelly Baby !

What do you get if you go on a blind date
wearing football boots ?

Stud up !

What do you get if you cross a
mad man and a bakery ?

Doughnuts !

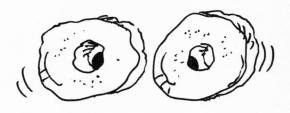

What do you get if you cross a
vampire and a bowl of soup ?

Scream of Tomato !

What do you get if you cross a pig and a laundry ?

Hogwash !

What do you get if you cross a cake and a disco ?

Abundance !

✎

What do you get if you cross a bad tempered witch
doctor, a fizzy drink and your dad ?

A bottle of pop !

✎

What do you get if you cross a dog and a film studio ?

Collie - wood !

✎

What do you get if you cross an insect and a dance ?

A cricket ball !

✎

What do you get if you cross a giant ape
and a self defence class ?

Kong - Fu !

What do you get if you cross a jet engine
and a tennis racket ?

A Tennis Rocket !

What do you get if you cross a sheep with a holiday
resort ?

The Baaahaaamaaas !

What do you get if you cross a sheep and a vampire ?

A were - wool !

What do you get if you cross a King and a boat ?

King Canoe !

What do you get if you cross a herb and
Doctor Who ?

A thyme machine !

What do you get if you cross two sailors and a
bottle of HP ?

Tartare Sauce !

What do you get if you cross a telephone
and a marriage bureau ?

A Wedding Ring !

What do you get if you cross a doctor's
surgery and a mountain range ?

Peak Practice !

What do you get if you cross a pig and an
emergency vehicle ?

A Hambulance !

What do you get if you cross a joke book
and a snowstorm ?

Corn Flakes !

What do you get if you cross a pig
and a telephone ?

A lot of crackling on the line !

What do you get if you cross a
vampire and a plumber ?

A drain in the neck !

What do you get if you cross an
Italian landmark and a ghost ?

The screaming tower of Pisa !

What do you get if you cross a
vampire with a mummy ?

Something you wouldn't want to unwrap !

What do you get if you cross a carrier pigeon
with a woodpecker?

A bird that knocks before delivering a message !

What do you get if you cross a frog
and a secret agent ?

A croak and dagger story !

What do you get if you cross a jellyfish
and an aircraft ?

A jelly copter !

What do you get if you cross a naked woman
and the bottom of the ocean ?

A deep sea Lady Godiva !

What do you get if you cross a singer and
a tall ladder ?

Someone who can easily get the high notes !

What do you get if you cross a
student and an alien ?

Something from another universe - ity !

What do you get if you cross an
alien and a hot drink ?

Gravi - tea !

What do you get if you cross a
mummy and a spaceship ?

Tutankha - moon !

What do you get if you cross a
gorilla and a prisoner ?

A Kong - vict !

AWFUL ALPHABET

Fan Belt –

Something that keeps a football
supporter's trousers up !

A

Aardvark — A vark that thinks it's tough !

Abdomen — Men with beer bellies !

Abigail — Strong wind heard in a monastery !

Absent minded — Oh ! I seem to have forgotten this one !?

Absolute — The best musical instrument in the World, ever !

Abundance — Disco for cakes !

Accidental — When you fall and knock your teeth out on the way to the dentists !

Angler — Someone who is good at maths !

Antifreeze — An Inuit's mum's sister !

Aromatic — Early machine for making arrows !

Astronaut - When a spaceman scores nothing in his maths exam !

Attendance - Dance for 10 people !

Audio Visual - Sign language !

Automate - When your best friend is a robot !

BEST®
BUD

B

Backgammon- Game played by pigs!

Baked Alaska- The result of global warming!

Balderdash - Running away from a crazy
hairdresser!

Bandsaws - Blisters on guitarist's fingers!

Barbecue - An outdoor party for sheep!

Bashful — Someone who has been in a fight !

Bathtub — Part of a fat man that never goes underwater in the bath !

Beckon — Send footballer on to the pitch !

Beehive — What *mummy* bees tell naughty bees to do !

Beeline — What naughty bees get at school!

Belladonna — Telephone a girl called Donna!

Bernadette — Set fire to your bills!

Betwixt — Halfway through a chocolate bar!

Big Top   - Large hat worn by circus ringmaster !

Bindweed   - Tie up a weak person !

Bird of Prey - Eagle that goes to church every Sunday !

Birkenhead   - Not very intelligent !

Blockade   - Stop lemonade being delivered !

Blood Brother - Vampire's relative !

Brain Wave   - Permed hair !

C

Cabinet Pudding – School pudding made from furniture !

Cagoule – Ghost's favourite raincoat !

Calculate – Finish maths test ages after everyone else !

Campus - Cat that lives in a college!

Capstan - Put Stan's hat on!

Carnivore - Animal that eats cars!

Carousel - Car that goes round in circles!

Cartoon - Song sung by cars!

Cat Burglar - Burglar who steals cats!

Caterpillar   - Where a cat sleeps !

Cauliflower   - Dog with a bunch of roses !

Celery   - Wages paid to a gardener !

Cheapskate - Skateboard for a budgie !

Chilli Powder- Fine snowflakes !

Christmas Island- Where Santa spends the Summer !

Chrysanthemum- Christopher and one parent !

Circumference- The knight who designed the round table !

Cliff Hanger - Where a giant leaves his coat !

Coarse fish - Bad mannered fish !

Coat of Arms- Monster's coat with 13 sleeves !

D

Dab Hand   – Someone who is very good at finger painting !

Daft   – Covered in daffodils !

Dandruff   – Mrs Druff's husband !

Dark Ages   – A time when there were lots of knights !

Deadline   – Fence around a graveyard !

Deception — The door that leads out of reception!

Deck Chair — Chair made from beach!

Defence — Something that runs round the garden!

Depend — The end of the swimming pool with most water!

Dessert Spoon — Spoon for eating sand!

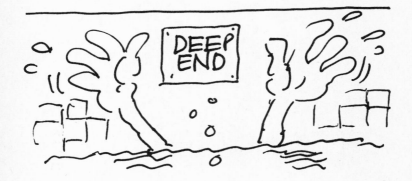

Diagnosis   - What you get from a Welsh doctor !

Disband   - Break up a pop group !

Disconcerted - Thrown out of a concert !

Dispense   - Give out pocket money !

Dissent   - Say you don't like someone's perfume !

Dogmatic   - Robot dog !

Dungarees   - Trousers worn for shifting manure !

E

Earwigs   - Hair that old people grow out of their ears !

Eclipse   - What the Martian gardener does with his hedges !

Editor   - Teacher who can throw chalk accurately over 25 metres !

Effortless   - Sleeping through an exam !

Elastic band – Group who play rubber
instruments !

I CAN REMEMBER
WHEN ALL THIS
WAS FIELDS ...

Elderberry – Oldest berry on the plant !

Electric Eel – Fish that swims in strong currents !

Emphasis – When your sister shouts at you !

Emulate – Ostrich pretending to be an Emu !

Engraving – Vampire's hobby !

Evaporated - Dried water - just add liquid!

Experiment - What scientists did 100 years ago and you are still doing in school!

Explosion - Result of experiment!

Eyecatching - Game played by monsters!

F

Factory   - Place where they make trees !

Fail Safe   - Safe with a broken lock !

Family Tree - Place where ghouls bury each
other for a laugh !

Fan Belt   - What a football supporter uses to
keep his trousers up !

Father In Law - Dad in jail !

Feed Back — When a vampire bites you from behind!

Fertile — Tiles in a werewolf's house!

Fetlock — Padlock for a horse!

Filbert — Give Albert his dinner!

Fireworks — Sack everybody in the factory!

Fish Fingers — What fish have 5 of on each hand!

Flagstone — Stone age Union Jack!

Flashback — What happens when you hold the camera back to front!

Flea Market — Where fleas do their shopping!

Flight Deck — The pack of cards used by pilots!

Fly by Night — Vampire Owl!

Flying Colours- Paint thrown in art lesson !

Flypaper   - What flies decorate their homes with !

Forward Roll - The 3 day old sandwich pushed to the front to make you buy it !

Foul Mouthed- Bad language from a chicken !

Four Poster - Bedroom with 4 posters on the wall !

Frog March - What frog soldiers do !

G

Galleon — Fuel measure for old ships !

Gamekeeper — Teacher who confiscates computer games in class !

Gargoyle — Pulling faces when gargling !

Generation Gap — The distance you keep behind your parents when they do something embarrassing, like dancing in supermarkets !

Gherkin   - Relatives of a Gher !

Gladiator   - How a monster felt after lunch !

Goal Mouth - Someone shouting from behind the nets !

Green Belt - Something which holds your pants up with recycled materials !

Gripe Water - The sort of rain that makes people complain !

H

Hacking Jacket – Coat worn for cutting hedges and trees!

Haggis – Eaten by witches in Scotland!

Hair Restorer – Vet!

Harvest – What farmers wear to cut corn!

Hatch Back – Car boot full of eggs!

Heart Warming - Monster's cooking class !

Heirloom - Weaving machine for rabbits !

Hog Wash - Pig in a bath !

Home Sick - Fed up being at home in the summer holidays !

Honeycomb - What bees use to style their hair !

Hoodwink   – What Robin Hood did to Maid Marian !

Hoot Owl   – Bird that doesn't care about anything !

Hopscotch – Sword dance in bare feet !

Humbug   – Insect that can't remember the words !

Hysterical   – Funny version of History !

I

Ice Cap — What your knee is when you fall on it when ice skating!

Identical — Twins who laugh at the same time when you tickle them!

Illiteracy — Disease caught from books!

Impeccable — Hidden away from birds!

Impediment - Broken bicycle !

Impersonate - Cannibals dinner guest !

Introduce - Orange drink served at start of match !

Italic - Italian smart alec !

J

Jackdaw — Lift a car up by the door handle !

Jam Packed — A car full of strawberry jam !

Jargon — A missing jar of strawberry jam !

Jelly Beans — What jelly babies have on toast !

Jitterbug — Tense insect !

Joan of Arc — Noah's mum !

Joint Account — The bank where Frankenstein keeps all his spare parts !

Juggernaut — Empty jug !

K

Karate   - Self defence for mice !

Kenya   - Can you ?

Kerb Drill   - Machine used for making holes in pavement !

Kerchief   - King of all the hankies !

Kettle Drum - What musicians make tea in !

Kidnap - Sleeping baby !

Kilocycle - Really hard bike to ride !

Kipper - Fish that is always asleep !

Korma - What you end up in if someone drops a pan of curry on your head !

L

Labrador — Large cat-flap for dogs !

Lady-In-Waiting— Woman in queue outside loo !

Lapdog — Greyhound used in racing !

Last Minute — Longest 60 seconds of the whole school day !

Laughing Stock - Funny Oxo cube !

Launch Pad - Throw notebook at someone !

Lazy Bones - Idle skeleton !

Lemon Squash - When an elephant sits down in a greengrocers !

Leopard Lily - A flower no-one wants to smell !

Lie Detector - Head teacher !

Linesman - Bad tempered teacher !

M

Magic Eye — What teachers have in the back of their heads !

Mental Cruelty — Double maths on Friday afternoon !

Metronome — Musical elf driving a Mini !

Microwave — Very small cooker !

Milk Chocolate - Something that no-one can do !

Milk Shake - What you get from nervous cows !

Misprint - Copy someone else's homework incorrectly !

Mistletoe - What Santa gets when he drops his sleigh on his foot !

Mitten - What a cat has when it swallows a ball of wool !

Moment of Truth- Exam results !

Mortar Board- What teachers who used to be bricklayers wear !

Mothball - What moths play football with !

Multi Storey - Very tall library !

Mummy - Egyptian child's daddy !

N

Narrow Minded - What you are when you have a splitting headache!

Near Miss - Avoid bullies by standing close to the teacher!

Neck Line - Vampire's target!

Neptune   - Song heard under water !

Nerve Cell   - Where naughty nerves are kept in prison !

Nick Name   - Steal someone's name !

Nightmare   - Vampire horse !

Night School - Vampire college !

SHIVER

BRRRRR

Nipper — Baby crab !

Numbskull — Very cold skeleton !

Nursery School — Where small plants go !

O

Octopus   – Cat born in October !

Odin   – Noisy God !

Off Cut   – Bad hairdo !

Opportune   – Music played on a pogo stick !

Optical   – Tickle an opera singer !

Organ Grinder - Monster with food processor !

Out Of Bounds - Escaped from prison !

Outside Broadcast - Shout through window !

Overcast - Throw fishing rod into middle of river !

Overgrown - Too big for last year's blazer !

P

Paddock   - Where horse ships dock !

Palatable   - Tasty table for monsters to eat !

Paperweight- Heavy school bag !

Parapet   - Pet parrot kept by parachutist !

Parity   - Two parrots exactly the same !

Partial Eclipse - Half trimmed hedge !

Password - Hand a note to someone in class !

Pebble Dash - Running with a stone in your trainer !

Pedigree - Degree for posh dogs !

Perch - Fish kept in a cage !

Perspex - Plastic spectacles !

Phoney — Fake mobile phone !

Physiotherapy — Medicine mixed with lemonade !

Picador — Select an entrance to a bullfight !

Pigment — Paints for pigs !

Pigswill — How a dead pig leaves things to his family !

Pillar Box — What posties sleep on at night !

Ping - Pong - Table tennis played by skunks !

Pizzicato - Pizza for cats !

Plasma - Mum made by a plastic surgeon !

Plus Fours - Trousers worn by maths teachers !

Po faced - The way you are supposed to look
reading serious poetry !

Pole Vault — Where the expensive poles are locked away !

Polygon — Missing parrot !

Polystyrene — Plastic parrot !

Pontoon — Song sung by card players !

Puddle — What you find on the pavement when it has been raining cats and dogs !

Punch Line — End of a boxing joke !

Q

Quadruped - Bicycle with 4 pedals !

Quicksand - Sand that runs away when you're
not looking !

Quicksilver - Money that's easy to spend !

Quiz master - Ask teacher questions he can't
answer !

R

Rag and Bone Man - Skeleton working in a clothes shop !

Rainbow   - Bow tie for a raindrop !

Raleigh   - Explorer who invented the bicycle !

Raspberry   - Very rude fruit !

Remorse   - Send coded signal again !

Reverse Charge- Telephone to stop herd of Rhinos squashing you !

Road Hog   - Pig driving badly !

Rush Hour   - When bullrushes go home from work

Rustler   - Woman in a tissue paper dress !

S

Sand Bank   - Where camels keep their savings !

Sandpaper   - Newspaper designed to be read on the beach !

Sapsucker   - Vampire who likes fools !

Satire   - Telling jokes sitting on a tall stool !

Saxophone   - Saxon telephone !

Scotch Egg – What you get from chickens fed on whisky !

Scrap Book – List of fights you've been in !

Scullery – Monster's kitchen !

Sharp Witted – Someone with a pointed head !

Shop Lifter – King Kong !

Siesta   - Car that never wakes up !

Skull Cap   - What a skull boy wears !

Slip Road   - Where it's icy enough to make a slide !

Snowball   - Formal do for snowmen and women !

Solar Flares - Trousers worn at space discos !

Sour Puss   - Cat that eats lemons !

Split Pea   - Pea with a split personality !

Sponge Cake - What jellyfish eat at parties !

Stale Mate   - Monster's friend !

Staple Diet   - Eating small bits of bent metal !

Steel Wool   - What you get from robot sheep !

Stereotype   - Type using two fingers !

Sticky Wicket - What bees leave after a cricket match !

T

Tadpole   – What a tad uses in pole vaulting !

Tangent   – Man who has been out in the sun !

Test Pilot   – Someone who makes paper aeroplanes out of his test paper !

Three Legged Race - What monsters win on their own !

Time Machine - Space ship full of herbs !

Toadstools - What a toad mends his car with !

Transparent - Glass mum or dad !

Trunk Call - Telephone an elephant !

Tuck Shop - Where Robin Hood first met Friar Tuck !

Tuning Fork - To make sure your musical chairs are all in tune !

U

Undercover - Spy hidden under your duvet !

Unearth   - When a vampire visits a friend !

Unlucky   - Running into a vampire when you are trying to escape from a werewolf !

Unmentionables - Censored !!

Unplug   - What you should do with an electric chair before you sit down !

V

Vaccination - A country where everyone has had a jab !

Vagabond - What you tie up a tramp with !

Vamoose - Run away from a ghostly elk !

Vampire Bat - What vampires play cricket with !

Vancouver - Garage !

Vulgar Fraction - A fraction with bad manners !

W

Watchdog — A dog that can tell the time !

Water Bed — Where crabs sleep !

Water Polo — What horses play in the swimming pool !

Water Table — Where fish eat their dinners !

Wear and Tear — What oversized monsters do with their clothes!

Weight Watcher - Someone who looks at his tum in the mirror all day long !

Wigwam - When your wig falls over your eyes and you walk into a lamp post !

Witch Craft - Broomstick !

Wolf Whistle - What a fox referee uses !

Wonkey - Unsteady Donkey !

Wrap - Music for mummies !

X - Y - Z

Xylophone — What you use to telephone someone on the planet Xylo !

X-Ray — The ghost of Ray !

Yankee Doodle — American Cartoonist !

Yellow Lines — What you get if you misbehave at traffic warden school !

Yolks   - Jokes told by chickens !

Youth Clubs - Cavemen's first weapon !

Zermatt   - What you wipe zer feet on !

Zinc   - Where you wash your face !

NUTTY NAMES

What do you call a man who forgets to put his underpants on?

Nicholas!

What do you call a man with a tree growing
out of his head ?

Ed - Wood !

What do you call a woman with a sheep on her head ?

Baa - Baa - Ra !

What do you call a man who
wears tissue paper trousers ?

Russell !

What do you call a nun with a washing machine on her head ?

Sister Matic !

Why did the man with a pony tail go to see his doctor ?

He was a little hoarse !

What do you call a witch flying through the skies ?

Broom Hilda !

How did the Prime Minister get to know the secret ?

Someone Blairted it out !

What did the idiot call his pet zebra ?

Spot !

What do you call a fish on the dining table ?

A Plaice Mat !

What do you call a man made from toilet paper ?

Louie !

What do you call a very tidy woman ?

Anita House !

What do you call a vampire that can lift up cars ?

Jack - u - la !

What do you call a vampire in a raincoat ?

Mack - u - la !

What do you call a vampire Father Christmas ?

Sack - u - la !

What do you call a girl who lives on the same street as a vampire ?

The girl necks door !

What do you call a picture painted by an old master ?

An Old Masterpiece !

What do you call a horse that eats Indian food ?

Onion Bha - gee - gee !

What do you call a vegetable that tells jokes ?

Jasper Carrot !

What do you call the coldest mammal in the World ?

The Blue Whale !

What do you call a dog that makes a bolt for the door ?

Blacksmith !

What do you call a man who steals cows ?

A beef burgler !

What do you call a man with a pile of soil on his head ?

Doug !

What do you call a man after he has
washed the soil off his head ?

Douglas !

What do you call a girl at a railway station ?

Victoria !

How does Posh Spice keep her husband under control ?

He's at her Beckham call !

What do you call an overweight vicar who plays football ?

The roly - poly - holy - goalie !

What do you call a woman with sandpaper on her head ?

Sandie !

What do you call her sister who lives at the seaside ?

Sandie Shaw !

What do you call the largest computer you can buy ?

A Big Mac !

What do you call medicine for horses ?

Cough stirrup !

What do you call a pretend railway ?

A play station !

What do you call a man with a kilt over his head?

Scott!

What do you call a man with a pig on his head?

Hamlet!

What do you call a man with eggs on his head?

Omelette!

What do you shout to the Frenchman
at the back of the race?

Camembert!

What do you call a poster advertising the
last teddy for sale in the shop ?

A one ted poster !

REDUCED

LAST
ONE

What do you call the dance that grown ups do
in the supermarket ?

The can-can !

What do you call a DJ lying across a horse's back ?

Jimmy Saddle !

What do you call a girl with a supermarket
checkout on her head ?

Tilly !

What do you call a mummy that washes up ?

Pharaoh liquid !

What do you call a Scottish racehorse rider ?

Jock - ey !

What do you call a pig with an itch ?

Pork scratching !

What do you call a rodent's carpet ?

A mouse mat !

What do you call a sweater that bounces ?

A Bungee Jumper !

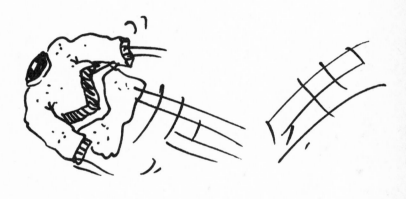

How do you spell hungry horse using just 4 letters ?

M T G G !

What do you call a woman dressed up as a gang of motor repairers ?

Car – men !

What do you call a Welshman who writes lots of letters ?

Pen Gwyn !

What sort of food can you get in a pub run by sheep ?

Baaa meals !

What do you call a female magician ?

Trixie !

What do you call well repaired holes in socks ?

Darned good !

What do you call a group made up of animal doctors ?

Vet, vet, vet !

What do you call a woman with a beach on her head ?

Shelly !

What do you call a postman with a cow on his head ?

Pat !

What do you call a woman who goes horse racing ?

Betty !

PHOTO FINISH

What do you call a woman who works in a bakers ?

Bunty !

What do you call a dinosaur that drinks PG Tips ?

A Tea Rex !

What do you call a deaf monster ?

Whatever you like - he can't hear you !

What do you call a vampire pig ?

Pork-U-La !

What do you call a man with a collection of fish photographs ?

The Prints of Whales !

(Yes, I know they're mammals really, but
I liked the joke anyway !)

What do you call a man with this book on his head?

Joe King!

What do you call a man with a football pitch
on his head?

Alf Time!

What do you call a man who cleans out toilets?

Lou!

What do you call a man
with the word LATER
painted on his head?

Ron (Later Ron!)

What do you call a woman with a bicycle on her head?

Petal!

What do you call a woman with a computerised
piano on the side of her head?

Cynthia!

What do you call a woman with a computerised
piano on top of her head?

Hyacinth!

What do you call a man with a load of sports
equipment on his head?

Jim!

What do you call a boy who is always making fun of people ?

Mickey !

What do you call a man with a load of flowers and vegetables growing on his head ?

Gordon !

What do you call a woman that people sit on ?

Cher !

What do you call a man with a spade on his head ?

Digby !

What do you call a woman with a boat on her head ?

Maude !

✎

What do you call a Roman emperor with flu ?

Julius Sneezer !

✎

What do you call a man with a sack full of stolen goods over his shoulder ?

Robin !

✎

What do you call a girl with a star on her head ?

Stella !

What do you call a mad man with the moon on his head ?

Lunar Dick !

What do you call a man with seagulls on his head ?

Cliff !

What do you call a secret store of food in a monastery ?

SECRET
GRUB
STORE

Friar Tuck

What do you call a man with a swarm of bees round his head ?

A. B. Hive !

What do you call a woman with a short skirt on ?

Denise !

What do you call a man with debts ?

Bill !

What do you call a woman who throws her bills on the fire ?

Bernadette !

What do you call a man who is part man, part jungle cat ?

Richard the Lion Half !

Why did the girl have a horse on her head ?

Because she wanted a pony tail !

What do you call a man
with a karaoke machine ?

Mike !

What do you call a man who checks the size
of rabbit holes ?

A Burrow Surveyor !

What do you call a woman with a nut tree on her head ?

Hazel !

What do you call a failed lion tamer ?

Claude Bottom !

What do you call a woman with a cat on her head?

Kitty!

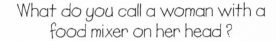

What do you call a woman with a
food mixer on her head?

Belinda!

What do you call a man who does everything in
30 seconds?

Arthur Minute!

What do you call a woman who is crunchy and thin ?

Crisp - tine !

What do you call a man who swings through
the jungle backwards ?

Nazrat !

What do you call a man who keeps chickens ?

Gregory Peck !

What do you call a man with a computer on his head ?

CD Ron !

What do you call a woman with a kettle on her head ?

Tina !

What do you call a disguise worn by an Elk ?

A False Moosetache !

What do you call a robbery in China ?

A Chinese Take Away !

What do you call a cat that is always having accidents ?

A Catastrophe !

What do you call two elephants at the swimming pool ?

A Pair Of Swimming Trunks !

What do you call a dog in a breadcake ?

A Hot Dog !

What do you call a teddies favourite drink ?

Ginger Bear !

What do you call a dance that snowmen go to ?

A Snowball !

What do you call the ring that worms leave
round the bath ?

The Scum Of The Earth !

What do you call a sheep that says Moo ?

Bilingual !

What do you call the flour that fairies make
bread with ?

Elf Raising Flour !

What do you call the highest form of animal life ?

A Giraffe !

What do you call a snake that's good at maths ?

An Adder !

What do you call a secret agent in a shop ?

A Counter Spy !

What do you call a ghost that lives in a bicycle wheel?

A Spook!

What do you call a buffalo that you can wash your hands in?

A Bison!

What do you call a man who jumps off a cliff with a budgie on each arm?

A Budgie Jumper!

What do you call the glasses a short sighted ghost wears?

Spooktacles!

What do you call something that runs around your garden all day and never stops ?

The Fence !

What do you call the place where the Police keep rhubarb thieves ?

Custardy !

What do you call a frog's favourite sweet ?

A Lollihop !

What do you call something that is green and
white and hops ?

A Frog Sandwich !

UGH ! That is so sick !

**Yes, and so was my dad when he opened
his packed lunchbox !**

✎

What do you call a holiday resort for bees ?

Stingapore !

✎

What do you call the song that monkeys
and elephants sing at Christmas ?

Jungle Bells !

What do you call a snail's favourite clothes ?

A Shell Suit !

What do you call a duck that's been to University ?

A Wise Quacker !

What do you call a baby turkey ?

A Goblet !

What do you call a rocking chair fitted with wheels ?

A Rock - And - Roller !

What do you call a pair of shoes made from banana skins ?

Slippers !

What do you call first aid for an injured lemon ?

Lemonade !

What do you call Tarzan when he visits Mars ?

Marzipan !

What do you call a fish that's eaten 24 carrots ?

A Gold Fish !

What do you call a fish that can't swim ?

Dead !

What do you call the King who invented the fireplace ?

Alfred the Grate !

What do you call a cat that's eaten a lemon?

A Sourpuss!

What do you say to an angry monster?

No need to bite my head off!

What do you call the longest night of the year?

A Fortnight!

What do you call a fast food snack served at a church fete?

A Hymn Burger!

What do you call a mayfly with criminal tendencies ?

Baddy long legs !

What do you call a ghost's songbook ?

Sheet Music !

What do you call a person who falls onto you
on a bus or train ?

A Laplander !

What do you call the World's first foot doctor?

William the Corncurer!

What do you call a holiday that rabbits go on when they first get married?

Bunnymoon!

What do you call a bull you can put in the washing machine?

Washable!

What do you call something purple that swings
through vineyards ?

Tarzan the grape man !

What do you call a person who shouts all the
way through a football match ?

A Foot bawler !

What do you call a fox in trouble with the police ?

A brush with the law !

What do you call a new, super cat ?

A Mew Improved Version !

ANIMAL ANTICS

What do you have when a rabbit sits on your head?

A Bad Hare day!

What weighs two and a half tons, is grey, and floats gracefully through the air?

A Hang Gliding Elephant!

What's the worst thing about being a millipede?

Washing your hands before tea!

A man went into a pet shop and asked the assistant if he could have a hamster for his son.

'Sorry, sir,' replied the assistant, 'we don't do part-exchanges.'

What did the earwig sing as it went to a football match?

Earwig - go, earwig - go, earwig - go....

What is worse than finding a slug in your salad sandwich?

Finding half a slug!

What do you call an 85 year old ant?

An antique!

What happens when there is a stampede
of cows on the motorway ?

There is udder chaos !

Where do you keep a pet vampire fish ?

In your blood stream !

Have you ever hunted bear ?

No, it's far too cold in this part of the world for that !

A cat just scratched my leg !

Shall I put some cream on it ?

No, it will be miles away by now !

✎

What is big and grey and has yellow feet ?

An elephant standing in custard !

✎

What is grey, has a trunk and travels at
125 miles an hour ?

A businessman on a fast train !

How did your budgie die?

Flu!

Don't be daft, budgies
can't die from flu!

**This one did - it flu
under a steam roller!**

What fish can you
see in the sky?

A Starfish!

Where do kippers go to be cured?

They go to the local sturgeon!

Waiter - this crab only has one claw!

Sorry, sir, it must have been in a fight!

**In that case, take this away and bring me
the winner!**

Doctor, doctor, I think I'm a cat !

How long have you felt like this ?

Since I was a kitten !

What time is it when an elephant sits on your fence ?

Time to get a new fence !

Doctor, doctor, I think I'm a crocodile !

Don't worry, you'll soon snap out of it !

Who won the headless horse race ?

No one, they both finished neck and neck !

What do you call a worm in a fur coat ?

A caterpillar !

Help, I've lost my cat !

Well, why don't you put an advert in the local newspaper ?

Don't be silly - cats can't read !

Eric, what is a prickly pear ?

Er....two porcupines ?!

Why do crabs walk sideways ?

**Because they had to take some medicine
which had side effects !**

What sort of insects don't know the words
to songs ?

Hum bugs !

..TUM-TE-TUM-TE-TUM....

A frog went to the doctor with a sore throat,
the doctor examined him and said...'you've got
a person in your throat !'

Where do ducks keep their savings ?

In river banks !

My dog often goes for a tramp in the woods - and the
tramp is getting a bit fed up with it !

What is the easiest way to get an elephant
to follow you home ?

Just act like a nut !

What do you call a dog that thinks it's a sheep ?

Baaaaaking mad !

What went into the lion's cage at the zoo and
came out without a scratch ?

Another lion !

First cow -   Are you worried about this mad
cow disease ?

**Second cow - Doesn't worry me,
I'm Napoleon Bonaparte !**

How do chimps make toast ?

Put it under a gorilla !

What goes bark, tick, bark, tick, bark, tick....

A watchdog !

✏

What is grey and highly dangerous ?

An elephant with a hand grenade !

✏

What did the dog say when its basket was
lined with sandpaper ?

Ruff, ruff !

How can you tell the difference between
an African elephant and an Indian elephant ?

Look at their passports !

How do you get when you cross a snake with
a magician ?

Abra - the - Cobra !

How many pigs do you need to make a smell ?

A Phew !

What is striped and keeps hearing a ringing sound ?

A zebra trapped in a telephone box !

What do ferrets have that no other creatures have ?

Baby ferrets !

What did the pig wear to the fancy dinner dance ?

A pig's - tie !

A man ran over a cat. He apologised to the owner and said that he would be happy to replace it !

**'How good are you at catching mice ?'
the owner asked him !**

How do you keep flies out of the kitchen ?

Put a load of manure in the dining room !

How can you cook chicken that really tickles the palate ?

Leave the feathers on !

How does a horse tell a joke ?

In a jockey - lar fashion !

What do pigs call bath night ?

Hog wash !

How many sheep does it take to make a woolly cardigan ?

I didn't know sheep could knit !

How do snails get ready for a special night out ?

They put on snail varnish !

What do you get if a whale sleeps in your bed ?

A wet duvet !

What is a grasshopper ?

A cricket on a pogo stick !

Which insect can stay underwater for hours at a time ?

A spider in a submarine !

Robert, you can't keep a pig in your bedroom - what about the terrible smell ?

Don't worry, he'll soon get used to it !

Why do kangaroos hate bad weather ?

Because the kids have to play inside !

Why was your dog growling at me all through the meal ?

Don't worry, he always does that when people use his favourite plate !

What do you shout to rabbits getting on a ship ?

Bun - voyage !

When is a stray cat likely to come into your home ?

When you leave the door open !

✎

Why did the girl have a pile of dirt on her shoulder ?

Because she had a mole on her cheek !

✎

Waiter, waiter, what is this spider doing in my salad ?

Looking for the flies we usually have in there !

✎

What happens when a frog breaks down ?

It gets toad away !

✎

How do you stop a skunk from smelling ?

Put a peg over its nose !

✎

What sort of animal are you never allowed to take into school exams ?

A Cheetah !

What's black and white and red ?

A zebra with nappy rash !

There's a stick insect in my salad - fetch me the branch manager at once !

How do you eat your turkey dinner ?

I just gobble it down !

Waiter, waiter, there's a button in my lettuce !

Ah ! That will be from the salad dressing sir !

What do monkeys do at the theatre ?

They ape - plaud !

Mmm ! This bread is lovely and warm !

It should be, the cat has been sitting on it all afternoon !

How do you find a lost dog ?

Make a noise like a bone !

They make a perfect couple - He has a chip on his shouder, and there's something fishy about her !

What sound does a Chinese frog make ?

Cloak !

Where does a six foot parrot sleep ?

Wherever it wants to !

Is that a bulldog ?

No, it's a Labrador, but it ran into a wall chasing a cat !

What sort of dog has no tail ?

A hot dog !

A man slipped when working on his roof, and was hanging onto the window ledge by his fingertips. He saw the cat through the window and called out to it to get help.

The cat said 'me ? how ?'

Why is a cat bigger at night than during the day ?

Because its owner lets it out at night !

What sort of jumpers do cows wear ?

Jerseys !

What do you get if you cross a skunk with a balloon ?

Something that stinks to high heaven !

What do cats read in the morning ?

The Mewspaper !

What did King Kong say when he was told that
his sister had had a baby ?

I'll be a monkey's uncle !

What did the skunk say when the wind
changed direction ?

It's all coming back to me know !

What game do cows play at birthday parties ?

Mooo - sical chairs !

What game do cats play at parties ?

Puss - the - parcel !

What game do fish play at parties ?

Sardines, what else !

What do you get if you cross a hippo with
a house sparrow ?

Massive holes in your roof !

Where would you find the skeleton of the very
first, prehistoric cow ?

In the Moooo-seum !

What did the sheep say to his girlfriend ?

I Love Ewe !

✎

What did the short sighted hedgehog say to
the cactus ?

Oh ! There you are mum !

✎

What do you call a woman with a frog on her head ?

Lily !

✎

What do you get if you cross a cow and a kangaroo ?

Something you need a trampoline to milk !

✎

What is grey, has 4 legs and a trunk ?

A mouse going on holiday !

✎

**Did you hear about the stupid farmer who took
his cows to the North Pole, thinking he would
get ice cream !**

What do you get if you cross a chicken with a dog ?

Pooched eggs !

What is the closest thing to silver ?

The Lone Ranger's saddle !

Look at those 50 cows over there !

I said, look at those 50 cows over there !!

Yes, I herd !

What sort of dog is good at looking after children ?

A Baby Setter !

What do the underwater police travel in ?

Squid cars !

Where do birds hold their coffee mornings ?

In a nest-cafe !

What sort of bird has fangs ?

Duckula !

What is hairy and writes ?

A ballpoint ferret !

What do you say to a hitch - hiking frog ?

Hop In !

I think your dog wants my dinner - he keeps jumping up at the table !

Well he didn't eat it this morning when I put it out for him so he'll have to do without now !

What do toads drink ?

Croaka Cola !

When do kangaroos propose ?

In Leap Years !

Why did the gorilla only eat one computer ?

Because he couldn't eat another byte !

What do you call someone who steals sheep ?

A Ram Raider !

Why is a real dog better than a cyberpet ?

Because your teacher will never believe you if
you tell him that your cyberpet buried your
homework in the garden !

How does the idiot call his dog ?

He puts both his forefingers in his mouth, takes
a deep breath, and shouts 'Here Boy.'

WHAT DO YOU CALL...

What do you call a scared biscuit ?

A Cowardy Custard Cream !

What do you call a man whose father was a Canon ?

A son of a gun !

What do you call a man with two left feet ?

**Whatever you like - if he tries to catch you
he'll just run round in circles !**

What do you call a weekly television programme about people getting washed?

A soap opera!

What do you call a flock of birds who fly in formation?

The Red Sparrows!

What do you call a bee who is always complaining?

A Grumble Bee!

What would you call a friend who had an elephant on his head?

A Flatmate!

What do you call a posh pig delivering newspapers ?

Bacon Rind !

What do you call a teacher who makes fireworks ?

A Head Banger !

What do you call a man who drills holes in teapots ?

A Potholer !

What do you call a song played on car horns ?

A Car Tune !

What do you call the man who invented a famous car and toilet paper ?

Lou Rolls !

What do you call an elephant that has had too much to drink ?

Trunk !

What do you call the owner of a tool factory?

The Vice Chairman!

What do you call King Midas when he stars in a James Bond film?

Goldfinger!

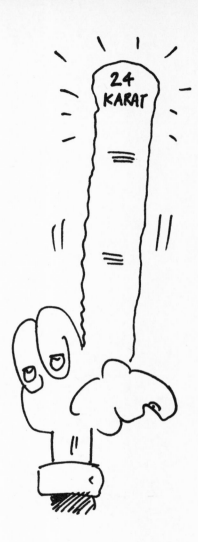

What do you call a parrot when it has dried itself after a bath?

Polly Unsaturated!

What do you call a dentist in the army?

A Drill Sergeant!

What do you call a Kangaroo at the North Pole ?

A Lost - Tralien !

What do you call a rabbit dressed up as a cake ?

A Cream Bun !

What do you call the man who went to a fancy dress
party as a sandwich ?

Roland Butter !

What do you call a man who rescues drowning
spooks from the sea ?

A Ghost Guard !

What do you call someone who makes half size
models of fish ?

A Scale Modeller !

What do you call someone who draws funny
pictures of motor vehicles ?

A Car - Toonist !

What do you call someone who dances on cars ?

A Morris Dancer !

What do you call a fight between film actors ?

Star Wars !

What do you call a group of cars ?

A Clutch !

What do you call a puzzle that is so hard it
makes people swear ?

A Crossword !

What do you call a dog that is always getting
into fights ?

A Boxer !

What do you call a witch's broomstick when you are very young ?

A Broom Broom !

What do you call a film about Mallards ?

A Duckumentary !

What do you call a musical instrument that is played by two teams of twenty people ?

A Piano Forte !

What do you call a very fast horse ?

Gee Gee Whizz !

What do you call the best dad in the world ?

Top of the Pops !

What do you call a chocolate that teases
small animals ?

A Mole - teaser !

What do you call a fish on a motorcycle ?

A Motor Pike !

What do you call a pen with no hair ?

A Bald Point !

What do you call a thing with 22 legs,
11 heads and 2 wings ?

A Football Team !

What do you call a cow that cuts grass ?

A Lawn Mooooooer !

What do you call a magical secret agent ?

James Wand !

What do you call it when an aeroplane
disappears over the horizon ?

Boeing, Going, Gone !

What do you call a hearing aid made from fruit ?

A Lemonade !

What do you call a policeman with blonde hair ?

A Fair Cop !

What do you call a 5-a-side match played
by chimney sweeps ?

Soot Ball !

What do you call a small parent ?

A Minimum !

What do you call a traffic warden who never fines anyone ?

A Triffic Warden !

What do you call a telephone call from one vicar to another ?

A Parson to Parson call !

What do you call the place where parrots make films ?

PollyWood !

What do you call a scared biscuit ?

A Cowardy Custard Cream !

What do you call an Igloo without a toilet ?

An Ig !

What do you call a superb painting done
by a rat ?

A Mouseterpiece !

What do you call a box of parrot food?

Polly Filla!

What do you call it when you pass out after eating too much curry?

A Korma!

What do you call a chicken that eats cement?

A Bricklayer!

POTTY POEMS

I cycled down to the burger bar,
Without my hands on the handlebars,
I lost control and broke my jaw,

I don't think I'll do that no more!

Mary had a little lamb,
and a little pony, too.
She put the pony in a field,
and the lamb into a stew !

Humpty Dumpty sat on a wall,
Humpty Dumpty had a great fall.
All the king's horses and
all the king's men,
thought it was really funny,
and asked him to do it again !

Simple Simon
met a pieman
going to the fair.
Said Simple Simon
to the pieman,
May I taste your wares ?
Said the pieman
to Simple Simon,
I don't sell wares
but you can try one of my pies if you like !

I wandered lonely as a cloud
that floats on high o'er hill and dell.
No-one would sit next to me
'cos I had made a nasty smell !

If you can pass exams,
while all about you are failing theirs,
you're a bigger swot than I am,
Gunga Din !

To be or not to be
that is the question,
or should I just use a pen instead !

Little Miss Muffet
sat on her tuffet
eating her favourite lunch.
A giant went by
looking up to the sky
and Little Miss Muffet went 'CRUNCH'

Little Bo-Peep
has lost all her sheep,
which is why she's down at the
job centre this morning !

I went to the pictures tomorrow
I got a front row seat at the back
I bought an ice cream with a cherry on top,
I ate it and gave it them back!

The animals went in two by two,
the elephant and the kangaroo,
the lion the tiger,
the cat and the dog,
the mouse the gorilla,
the rat and the frog,
but they could only find one dinosaur,
which is why they aren't around any more!

Little Jack Horner,
sat in the corner,
eating his apple pie.
he put in his thumb,
and pulled out a plum,
and said 'that's a
funny looking apple!'

Hickory Dickory Dock,
6 mice ran up the clock.
The clock struck one,
but the other 5
got away!

Jack and Jill
went up the hill
to fetch a pail of water,
Jack fell down
and broke his crown
and Jill said
I told you you shouldn't
try and skateboard down...

A green spotted alien from Mars
liked eating motorcycles and cars.
When people cried 'shame'
he said 'It's the same...
as you lot eating Mars bars !'

At lunchtime every schoolday,
Blenkinsop (the fat),
would eat his way through everything,
except the kitchen cat.
Two plates of chips, for starters,
a pack of crisps (or three),
then on to shepherds pie and beans,
washed down with mugs of tea.
Spaghetti Bolognese and rice,
it all went down a treat,
Chicken curry, very nice,
pasties (cheese and meat).
When all the savouries had been,
dispatched into his belly,
he started on the sweet menu,
(say goodbye to the jelly!)
Rice pudding, jam and eccles cakes,
yogurt, custard, shortbread,
till suddenly he simply burst,
on the final slice of bread.

When Mary had a little lamb
the doctor was surprised,
but when Old Macdonald had a farm
he couldn't believe his eyes !

School, glorious school,
we love all our teachers,
our lessons are cool,
but some pupils are creatures.

I never could,
quite work out why,
an elephant,
could never fly.
With massive ears,
to flap and twitch,
you'd think they'd glide
without a hitch.

BATTY BRAIN TEASERS

Why did the hen cross the road ?

To prove she wasn't chicken !

What do you call a man with a tree growing
out of his head ?

Ed - Wood !

How do you stop a head cold going to your chest ?

Easy - tie a knot in your neck !

Why shouldn't you try to swim on a full stomach ?

Because it's easier to swim on a full swimming pool !

What creature sticks to the bottom of sheep ships ?

Baaa - nacles !

How do you know if your little brother is turning into a 'fridge?

See if a little light comes on whenever he opens his mouth!

What is the coldest part of the North Pole?

An explorer's nose!

What do computer operators eat for lunch?

Chips!

Why is that man standing in the sink ?

He's a tap dancer !

Where do rabbits learn to fly ?

In the Hare Force !

How did the witch know she was getting better ?

**Because the doctor let her get
out of bed for a spell !**

What did the witch call her baby daughter ?

Wanda !

How do witch children listen to stories ?

Spellbound !

'Which witch went to Ipswich ?
The rich witch called little Mitch,
with the light switch for the soccer pitch,
who twitched and fell in a ditch;
that witch went to Ipswich -
and never came home !

What would you find in a rabbit's library ?

Bucks !

Why can you never swindle a snake ?

Because it's impossible to pull its leg !

What did the overweight ballet dancer perform ?

The dance of the sugar plump fairy !

Why is it easy to swindle a sheep ?

Because it is so easy to pull the wool over its eyes !

What do elves eat at parties ?

Fairy Cakes !

What do you get if you cross a brain surgeon
and a herd of cows ?

Cow-operation !

Why did the carpenter go to the doctor ?

He had a saw hand !

What is the only true cure for dandruff ?

Baldness !

What should you buy if your hair falls out ?

A good vacuum cleaner !

A man went to see his doctor with a brick buried
in his head. What was he suffering from ?

Falling arches !

Why did the doctor operate on the man who swallowed a pink biro ?

He had a cute-pen-inside-is !

Nurse - why are you putting Mr Smith's left leg in plaster, it's his right leg that's broken ?!

It's OK, I'm new so I'm practising on the left one first to make sure I do it properly!

What sort of fish would you find in a bird cage ?

A Perch !

What sort of fish would you find in a shoe ?

An Eel !

What sort of dance do fish do at parties ?

The Conga !

Where did the dog breeder keep his savings ?

In bark-lays bank !

Did you hear about the bungee jumper who shot up and down for 3 hours before they could bring him under control ?

He had a yo-yo in his pocket !

What do you call a cowboy who helps out in a school?

The Deputy Head!

What do you call the teacher in the school who gives out forms that you have to fill in?

The Form Teacher!

Did you hear about the dog who was arrested?

He didn't pay a barking ticket!

Where did the rich cat live ?

In a mews cottage !

What position did the witch play in the football team ?

Sweeper !

What position did the pile of wood play in the football team ?

De-fence !

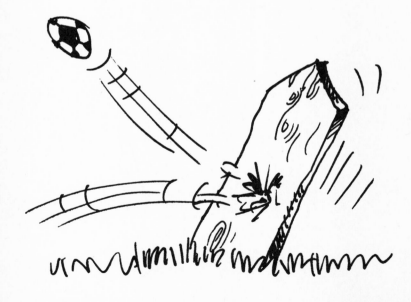

Why couldn't the slow boxer get a drink at the party ?

Because everyone beat him to the punch !

Why was the archaeologist upset ?

His job was in ruins !

Why was the butcher worried ?

His job was at steak !

Why did the teacher have to turn the lights on ?

Because his pupils were so dim !

Why did the French farmer only keep the one chicken ?

Because in France one egg is un oeuf !

What did the farmer say when all his cows
charged him at once ?

I'm on the horns of a dilemma here !

What sort of snake will tell on you ?

A grass snake !

Why did the doll blush ?

Because she saw the Teddy Bear !

POINTLESS INVENTIONS...

Camouflage for stick insects !

Disposable rubbish bags !

Colour radio !

Invisible traffic lights !

Plastic tea bags !

Waterproof soap !

Fireproof petrol !

WHERE ARE THE DISPOSABLE RUBBISH BAGS ?

I'VE THROWN THEM AWAY

What sort of ring is always square ?

A boxing ring !

What sort of queue is always straight ?

A snooker cue !

What sort of net is useless for catching fish ?

A football net !

Why do people leave letters at the football ground ?

They want to catch the last goal-post !

I've got a terrible fat belly !

Have you tried to diet ?

Yes, but whatever colour I use it still looks fat !

What do you call a
frog that helps
children safely
across the street ?

The green cross toad !

Did you hear about
the posh chef
with an attitude
problem ?

**He had a french
fried potato on
his shoulder !**

Why do golfers carry a spare sock?

Because they might get a hole in one!

A rather dim gardener from Leeds,
once swallowed a packet of seeds.
In just a few weeks,
his ears turned to leeks,
and his hair was a tangle of weeds!

I once met a man from Hong Kong,
who'd been jogging for twenty years long.
He was terribly sweaty,
- he looked like a yeti,
and his feet had a terrible pong!

What book do you buy to teach children
how to fight ?

A scrapbook !

What sort of animals make the best TV presenters ?

Gnus - readers !

What sort of animal is best at getting up
in the morning ?

A LLama clock !

I hear you've just invented gunpowder ?

Yes, I was using some candles to light my laboratory and it came to me in a flash !

How is your other invention coming along –
you know, the matches ?

Oh ! They've been a striking success !

Why did the doctor take his nose to pieces ?

He wanted to see what made it run !

Why is it dangerous
to tell jokes to
Humpty Dumpty ?

He might crack up !

Blenkinsop - stop acting the fool -
I'm in charge of this class, not you !

Why do pens get sent to prison ?

To do long sentences !

What was the parrot doing in prison ?

It was a jail-bird !

What is the name of the detective who sings quietly to himself while solving crimes ?

Sherlock Hums !

Why did the farmer feed his pigs sugar and vinegar ?

He wanted sweet and sour pork !

What do you call the Scottish dentist ?

Phil McCavity !

Why is the soil in my garden always dry ?

Because you have leeks !

What kind of rose
has a bark ?

A dog rose !

What did the little
boy say when he
wanted his big
brother to give him
back his building
bricks ?

Lego !

Why are you called
Postman Pat ?

**Because I have to
deliver post to all
the farms !**

Which two words
in the English
language have the
most letters ?

Post Office !

How do you start a jelly baby race ?

Ready - Set - Go !

What sort of music was invented by fish ?

Sole music !

What gets smaller the more you put in it ?

A hole in the ground !

Waiter, why is there a dead fly in my soup ?

**Well, you surely don't expect to get
a live one at these prices !**

What happened to the man who
stole a lorry load of eggs ?

He gave himself up - he said he only did it for a yolk !

Stop ! This is a one-way street !

Well, I'm only going one way !?

Yes, but everyone else is going the other way !

Well, you're a policeman, make them turn round !

What is the thing that is most red at Christmas ?

Rudolph's nose !

How do penguins get to school?

On 21 speed mountain icicles!

Why do cows have horns?

Because they would look pretty silly
with bells on their heads!

Mary had a little lamb,
which she dressed in pretty blouses,
she also had a ferret,
which she put down her dad's trousers!

What goes MOOOOOZ ?

A jet flying backwards !

What do blacksmiths eat for breakfast ?

Vice Crispies !

Why do toolmakers always escape from fires ?

They know the drill !

What self defence method do mice use ?

Ka - rat - e !

What did the stupid burglar do when he saw
a 'WANTED' poster outside the police station?

He went in and applied for the job!

What is a big game hunter?

Someone who can't find the football stadium!

30 people were sheltering under an umbrella,
how many of them got wet ?

None - it wasn't raining !

Why are burglars such good tennis players ?

**Because they spend such a lot of their time
in courts !**

Is that a new perfume I smell ?

It is, and you do !

What do vampires use to 'phone relatives ?

A terror - phone !

What are wasps favourite flowers ?

Bee - gonias !

Why did the fly fly ?

Because the spider spied her !

✎

What sort of monster is musical ?

The one with A Flat head !

✎

Where do Chinese vampires live ?

Fang - Hai !

Why did the Romans build straight roads ?

They didn't want anyone hiding round the corners !

✎

What do you call a dinosaur that
keeps you awake at night?

Bronto - snore - us !

✎

What is the name of the Australian dog drummer ?

Dingo Starr !

GHASTLY GHOSTS

Why do window cleaners hate vampires ?

They are a pane in the neck !

Which window cleaners do vampires use ?

The one in pane - sylvania !

Why do monsters like to stand in a ring ?

They love being part of a vicious circle !

What do you call a ghostly teddy bear ?

Winnie the OOOooooooOoooohhHHhhhhh !

Why did the vampire go to
the blood donor centre ?

To get lunch !

What do you call a Welsh ghost ?

Dai !

What do you call a tough Welsh ghost that
stars in an action movie ?

Dai Hard !

Why did the England cricket team consult a vampire ?

They wanted to put some bite into the opening bats !

How do vampires start a duel?

They stand Drac to Drac!

When do ghosts wear red jackets and ride horses?

When they go out fox haunting!

Why are owls so brave at night?

Because they don't give a hoot for ghosts, monsters or vampires!

What did the old vampire say when he broke his teeth ?

Fangs for the memory !

Why do vampires holiday at the seaside ?

They love to be near the ghostguard stations !

What is the ghostly Prime Minister called ?

Tony Scare !

What do you call a dentist who really likes vampires ?

An extractor fan !

What do you call a
futuristic android
who comes back in
time to plant seeds ?

Germinator !

And what do you
call his twin brother ?

Germinator II !

What do you call the ghost of the handkerchief ?

The Bogie man !

What sort of wolf can you wear ?

A wear wolf !

What sort of wolf delivers Christmas presents ?

Santa Claws !

What do you call a lazy skeleton ?

Bone Idle !

What do you call a ghostly would-be Scottish King ?

Boney Prince Charlie !

Why do ghosts catch cold so easily ?

They get chilled to the marrow !

What do you call a scary, boney creature that
staggers around making strange wailing noises?

A supermodel making a record!

Why are skeletons no good at telling lies?

Because you can see right through them!

What should you say when a vampire
gives you a present?

Fang you very much!

Why don't vampires like modern things ?

Because they hate anything new fangled !

✎

Why did the ghost get the job he applied for ?

He was clearly the best candidate !

✎

What do you call a ghostly haircut with long curly
strands of hair ?

Deadlocks !

✎

What do ghosts like
with their food ?

A little whine !

What film is about a scary train robber?

Ghost Buster!

Where do ghosts live?

In flats!

Where do vampires like to go for their holidays?

The Dead Sea!

Why did the two vampire bats get married?

Because they were heels over heads in love!

What did the pirate get when he smashed
a skeleton up in a fight ?

A skull and very cross bones !

Where do skeletons cook their meals ?

In a skullery !

What do you call a young
skeleton in a cap and uniform ?

A skullboy !

Why did the skeleton fall into a hole?

It was a grave mistake!

What villain does the spooky 007 fight?

Ghoulfinger!

Why are hyenas always falling out?

They always have a bone to pick with each other!

Who delivers Christmas presents to vampires?

Sack-ula!

What vampire can you wear to protect
you from the rain?

Mac - ula!

What is the fairy tale about a girl who
falls in love with a really ugly loaf of bread?

Beauty and the yeast!

When they got married, what sort of children
did they have?

Bun-shees!

Why did Goldilocks go to Egypt?

She wanted to see the mummy bear!

AND, SPEAKING OF MUMMIES...

Mummy, mummy, what is a vampire ?

Be quiet and eat your soup before it clots !

Mummy, mummy, what is a werewolf ?

Be quiet and comb your face !

Mummy, mummy
I don't like my
uncle Fred !

**Well, just leave
him on the side
of your plate
and eat
the chips !**

Mummy, mummy I don't want to go to America !

Be quiet and keep swimming !

Mummy, mummy I'm just going out for a quick
bite to eat !

**OK, but make sure you're back in your
coffin before daybreak !**

✏️

What did the monster say when the vampire asked for
his daughter's hand in marriage ?

OK, we'll eat the rest !

✏️

Why do some ghosts paint themselves
with black and white stripes ?

So they can frighten people on Pelican crossings !

OR

So they can play for Boocastle United !

What should you wear when you go out
for a drink with a vampire ?

A metal collar !

What do you call a young woman who hunts vampires ?

A Miss Stake !

What do the police call it when they
watch a vampire's house ?

A stake out !

What does the monster Tarzan eat for tea ?

Snake and pygmy pie with chips !

What did the ghostly show jumper always score ?

A clear round !

What did the young ghost call his mum and dad ?

His trans-parents !

Why don't you have
to worry what you
say to the werewolf
computer engineer ?

**His bark is worse
than his byte !**

What sort of jokes do werewolves like best ?

Howlers !

What happens when a werewolf meets a vampire ?

He doesn't turn a hair !

Why wasn't the werewolf allowed to get
off the lunar spaceship ?

Because the moon was full !

Why did the werewolf start going to the gym ?

Because he liked the changing rooms !

CHANGING

What did the train driver say to the werewolf ?

Keep the change !

Why did the werewolf steal underwear
when the moon was full ?

**Because his doctor told him a change
was as good as a vest !**

What sort of news do werewolves fear ?

Silver bulletins !

Why did the shy werewolf hide in a cupboard
every full moon ?

Because he didn't like anyone to see him changing !

What form of self defence do werewolves use ?

Coyote !

How do mummies knock on doors ?

They wrap as hard as they can !

Why was the mummy done up in brightly coloured sparkly
paper ?

He was gift-wrapped !

What does it say on the *mummy's* garage entrance ?

Toot, and come in !

What do *mummies* use to fasten things together ?

A Hammer and Niles !

What do children in Egypt call their parents ?

Mummy and Daddy of course !

Why was the Egyptian Prince worried ?

Because his *mummy* and daddy were both *mummies* !

What do mummies shout when they are on a sinking boat ?

A bandage ship !

What do mummies do to relax ?

They just unwind a little !

Why was the *mummy's* leg stiff ?

Because someone had been winding him up !

What are the scariest dinosaurs?

Terror dactyls!

Why are mummies good
at keeping secrets?

**They can keep things
under wraps for
centuries!**

Why did the werewolf
go out at the
full moon?

**Because his doctor
told him that a
change would
do him good!**

What did the ghost
of the owl say?

**Too-wit too-
woooooooooooo....**

Why is Godzilla sitting on a friend like leaving home ?

Because you end up with a flat mate !

✏

Who was the winner of the headless horse race ?

No-one, they all finished neck and neck !

✏

What did the President of the USA say to the giant ape when he won the lottery?

Kong - ratulations !

What eats your letters when you post them ?

A ghost box !

What spook delivers your letters ?

Ghostman Pat and his skeleton cat !

Which creature saves people from drowning ?

The Ghostguard !

Why did the vampire like eating chewy sweets ?

He liked something to get his teeth into !

Why do sausages and bacon spit when
they are being cooked ?

Because it's a terror frying experience !

What is the scariest thing you could find in your
Christmas stocking ?

The ghost of Christmas presents !

Why did the vampire put tomato ketchup
on his sandwiches ?

He was a vegetarian !

How do you grow a werewolf from a seed ?

Just use plenty of fur-tiliser !

Why can you never get through to a vampire
bat on the telephone ?

Because they always hang up !

What football teams does Dracula support ?

Shiverpool !

Fang-chester United !

Scream Park Rangers !

What football team does Frankenstein's
monster support ?

Bolt - On Wanderers !

What is a werewolf's favourite film?

The Full Moonty!

What lies at the bottom of the sea and shivers?

A nervous wreck!

Which vampire likes playing practical jokes?

Dracu-lark!

Where do vampires keep their savings?

In a blood bank or the ghost office!

What did Jeremy Paxman say to the werewolf
team on University Challenge ?

No con-furring !

What pop group did the young mummies join ?

A boy bandage !

What would you call a mummified cat ?

A first aid kit !

Why was Dracula ill
after biting someone
on a train home
from work ?

**He caught a
commuter virus !**

If hairy palms is the first sign of turning into
a monster, what is the second ?

Looking for them !

How do you stop a werewolf attacking you ?

Throw a stick for it to fetch !

What was on the haunted aeroplane ?

An air ghostess and a lot of high spirits !

Why couldn't the ghost get a whisky
in the pub after 11 o'clock ?

**Because they aren't allowed to serve
spirits after closing time !**

Why did the witch take her small
book of magic on holiday ?

The doctor told her to get away for a little spell !

Who was the fattest mummy ever ?

Two ton Carmen !

Why couldn't the witches victim move ?

He was spellbound !

How can you spot a sea monster ?

He's the one with the wavy hair !

What do sea monsters eat ?

Fish and ships !

Why do sea monsters go to so many parties ?

They like to have a whale of a time !

Which sea monster rules the waves ?

The Cod-father !

What do baby sea monsters play with ?

Doll-fins !

What do you give a monster that feels sick ?

Plenty of room !

Where do monsters sleep ?

Anywhere they want to !

What do you get if a monster falls over in a car park ?

Traffic jam !

What would you get if you combined a monster,
a vampire, a werewolf and a ghost?

As far away as possible !

What do monsters call a crowded swimming pool ?

Soup !

✎

What do you get if you shoot a werewolf with a silver bullet ?

A very interesting rug !

✎

What do you call the ghost of a werewolf that lives at the seaside ?

A Clear - Pier - Were - Wolf !

✎

How did Frankenstein's monster escape from the police ?

He made a bolt for it !

✎

Why did Dracula visit a psychiatrist ?

He thought he was going batty !

What sort of music do vampires and ghosts like best ?

Haunted House Music !

If a monster buys you a chair for your birthday
should you accept it ?

Yes - but don't let him plug it in !

What does a monster shout when it is scared ?

Mummy !

Can you stick vampires to your window ?

Yes - they are suckers !

Why did the ghost go to the bicycle shop ?

He needed some new spooks for his front wheel !

Where do ghouls live ?

Bury !

What game do ghouls play ?

Bury St Edmonds !

What do you call a stupid vampire ?

A clot !

What sort of jobs do spooks like ?

Dead end jobs !

What do ghosts do at parties ?

They have a wail of a time !

Who do vampires invite to their birthday parties ?

Anybody they can dig up !

Why don't ghosts go out during the day ?

They are scared of people !

Why don't skeletons have glass eyes ?

Because they come out in conversation !

Why are vampires always cheerful ?

Because they are terrified of being cross !

What is a werewolves favourite film ?

Claws !

What sort of voice do werewolves have ?

Husky ones !

What do werewolves hate most ?

When people lead them a dog's life !

What do you get if you cross a vampire with
a knight of the round table ?

A Bite in shining armour !

What was Dr Frankenstein best at ?

Making new friends !

What do spooks eat in the morning ?

A hearty breakfast of Dreaded Wheat !

Why didn't the vampire laugh at the joke
about the wooden stake ?

He didn't get the point !

What do you get if you cross the Abominable
Snowman and Count Dracula ?

Severe frostbite !

Where do spooks go shopping ?

In BOOOO-tiques !

What did the spook begin his letter with ?

Tomb it may concern....

Where is the invisible man ?

No idea, I haven't seen him around for ages !

What did the sign in the pyramid shop say ?

Satisfaction guaranteed or your mummy back !

Why are vampires so thin?

They eat necks to nothing!

Why did the ghoul take so long
to finish his newspaper?

He wasn't very hungry!

Why did the monster eat a settee and two
armchairs?

He had developed a suite tooth!

Why did the vampire bats hangingin the
church belfry look exactly the same
as each other ?

They were dead ringers !

Why didn't the spook win the lottery ?

He didn't have a ghost of a chance !

Why did the ghost of Guy Fawkes go crazy ?

It's OK, he just lost his head for a moment !

Wow - did you see that wolf ?

Where ?

No - it was just an ordinary one !

What sport do monsters like best ?

Sculling !

How do you know when there is a horrible monster under your bed ?

You don't - that's what makes it so very scary !

KNOCK, KNOCK...

Knock, knock...
Who's there?
Bea...
Bea Who?
Bea good boy and let me in!

Knock, knock...
Who's there ?
Yula...
Yula Who ?
Yula pologise for not letting me in straight
away when you see who it is !

Knock, knock...
Who's there ?
CD's...
CD's Who ?
CD's fingers ? They're freezing - let me in !

Knock, knock...
Who's there ?
Wyatt...
Wyatt Who ?
**Wyatt you open the
door and see !**

Knock, knock...
Who's there ?
Ivan...
Ivan Who ?
**Ivan idea you will know
as soon as you
open the door !**

Knock, knock...
Who's there ?
Toyah...
Toyah Who ?
**Toyah have to ask
the same question
every time I come
round ?**

Knock, knock...
Who's there ?
Wynn...
Wynn Who ?
Wynn de Cleaner !

Knock, knock...
Who's there ?
Willy...
Willy Who ?
Willy lend me a street map, I'm a stranger in town !

Knock, knock...
Who's there ?
Bea...
Bea Who ?
Bea good boy and let me in !

Knock, knock...
Who's there ?
Stan...
Stan Who ?
Stan in front of the window and you'll see who !

Knock, knock...
Who's there ?
The Steps...
WOW - you mean the hit band ?
No, just the steps up to your front door !

Knock, knock...
Who's there ?
Paul...
Paul Who ?
**Paul the door open a
bit, my coat is
trapped !**

Knock, knock...
Who's there ?
Irma...
Irma Who ?
**Irma little short of
time - just open up !**

Knock, knock...
Who's there ?
Carrie...
Carrie Who ?
**Carrie on like this and I'll have frozen
to death before I get in !**

Knock, knock...
Who's there ?
Fred...
Fred Who ?
Fred you'll have to open the door to find out !

Knock, knock...
Who's there ?
Vidor...
Vidor Who ?
Vidor better open soon....!

Knock, knock...
Who's there ?
Cole....
Cole Who ?
Cole out here - open up !

Knock, knock...
Who's there ?
Curley...
Curley Who ?
**Curley self a good host -
keeping your guests
waiting out here !**

Knock, knock...
Who's there ?
Ashley...
Bless you !

Knock, knock...
Who's there ?
Freda...
Freda Who ?
Freda jolly good fellow...

Knock, knock...
Who's there ?
Holly...
Holly Who ?
Holly up and open the door, I'm fleezing out here !

Knock, knock...
Who's there ?
Piers...
Piers Who ?
**Piers I've forgotten my
key - open up, there's a good chap !**

Knock, knock...
Who's there ?
Julian...
Julian Who ?
**Julian on that door all day waiting for
people to knock?**

Knock, knock...
Who's there ?
Major...
Major Who ?
Major ask that question yet again didn't I !

Knock, knock...
Who's there ?
Sara...
Sara Who ?
Sara man delivering milk here yesterday - do you think he could deliver some to me too ?

Knock, knock...
Who's there ?
Joe...
Joe Who ?
Joe keep everybody waiting like this ?

Knock, knock...
Who's there ?
Tia...
Tia Who ?
Tia mount of time I've wasted standing here...!

Knock, knock...
Who's there ?
Norm...
Norm Who ?
**Norm more Mr Nice Guy –
OPEN THIS DOOR !**

Knock, knock...
Who's there ?
Giraffe...
Giraffe Who ?
Giraffe to ask such stupid questions ?

Knock, knock...
Who's there ?
Doctor...
Doctor Who ?
You've played this game before, haven't you ?

Knock, knock...
Who's there ?
Alpaca...
Alpaca Who ?
**Alpaca suitcase and leave you if you
don't give me my own key !**

Knock, knock...
Who's there ?
Paula...
Paula Who ?
**Paula door open for me, I've got
my hands full of shopping bags !**

Knock, knock...
Who's there ?
Postman Pat...
Have you got a parcel ?
No, but I've got a black and white cat !

Knock, knock...
Who's there ?
London's...
London's who ?
**Ah ! You cheated ! I'll bet you can hear
the animals from there !**

Knock, knock...
Who's there ?
Lizard...
Lizard Who ?
Lizard - dobn't get too close, I'b
got a tebbible cold !

Knock, knock...
Who's there ?
Carib...
Carib Who ?
Was it the antlers that gave it away ?

Knock, knock...
Who's there ?
Denise...
Denise Who ?
Denise are freezing in this short skirt !

Knock, knock...
Who's there ?
Isiah...
Isiah Who ?
Isiah than you – I'm up on the roof !

Knock, knock...
Who's there ?
Carla...
Carla Who ?
Carla doctor – I feel terrible !

Knock, knock...
Who's there ?
Mandy...
Mandy Who ?
Mandy with tools, if you need any repair work done !

Knock, knock...
Who's there ?
The Electricity Board also known as the George...
The Electricity Board also known as the George Who ?
**The Electricity Board also known as the
George of the light brigade !**

Knock, knock...
Who's there ?
Pop...
Pop Who ?
Pop down and unlock this door please !

Knock, knock...
Who's there ?
Jim...
Jim Who ?
**Jim mind not asking the same old question
over and over !**

Knock, knock...
Who's there ?
Carter...
Carter Who ?
Carter a long story short and open up !

Knock, knock...
Who's there ?
Alison...
Alison Who ?
Alison at the keyhole sometimes...

Knock, knock...
Who's there ?
I Santa...
I Santa Who ?
I Santa message that I would
be here hours ago -
why is the door still locked ?

Knock, knock...
Who's there ?
Twit...
Twit who ?
Oh! Have you got a pet owl as well ?

Knock, knock...
Who's there ?
Ron...
Ron who ?
Ron away as fast as you can,
the aliens are coming...!

Knock, knock...
Who's there ?
It's Lewis...
It's Lewis who ?
It's Lewis this door knob...I should get it fixed !

Knock, knock...
Who's there ?
Card...
Card who ?
Card seem to get my key to work in this lock !

Knock, knock...
Who's there ?
Tai Ping...
Tai Ping who ?
Tai Ping these jokes is making my fingers ache !

Knock, knock...
Who's there ?
Noah...
Noah who ?
Noah anywhere I can shelter from this rain ?

Knock, knock...
Who's there ?
Yvonne...
Yvonne who ?
Yvonne to know you should open the door !

Knock, knock...
Who's there ?
Alpaca...
Alpaca who ?
Alpaca lunchbox for the train journey !

Knock, knock...
Who's there ?
Opera...
Opera who ?
**Opera sock in it and open
the door for goodness sake !**

Knock, knock...
Who's there ?
Carrie...
Carrie who ?
**Carrie on like this and I'll be frozen to death
before you open the door !**

Knock, knock...
Who's there ?
Alec...
Alec who ?
Alec the smell of fried egg and bacon
coming from your kitchen !

Knock, knock...
Who's there ?
Marge...
Marge who ?
Marge over to this door and open it, now !

Knock, knock...
Who's there ?
Lou...
Lou who ?
**There's no need to cry - I just
want to come in !**

Knock, knock...
Who's there ?
Carmen...
Carmen who ?
Carmen let me in please !

Knock, knock...
Who's there ?
Isiah...
Isiah who ?
Isiah than you, cos I'm standing on a box !

Knock, knock...
Who's there ?
Dinnah...
Dinnah who ?
Dinnah keep me waiting oot here its freezin !

Knock, knock...
Who's there ?
Les...
Les who ?
Les read this book again, it's brilliant !